Penguin Readers

THE EXTRAORDINARY LIFE OF MICHELLE OBAMA

DR SHEILA KANANI

T0190630

LEVEL

3

ADAPTED BY ANNE COLLINS
ILLUSTRATED BY SARAH WALSH
SERIES EDITOR: SORREL PITTS

Many of the quotes in this book have been simplified
for learners of English as a foreign language.

PENGUIN BOOKS

UK | USA | Canada | Ireland | Australia
India | New Zealand | South Africa

Penguin Books is part of the Penguin Random House group of companies
whose addresses can be found at global.penguinrandomhouse.com.

www.penguin.co.uk www.puffin.co.uk www.ladybird.co.uk

The Extraordinary Life of Michelle Obama first published by Puffin Books, 2019
This Penguin Readers edition published by Penguin Books Ltd, 2020

002

Original text written by Dr Sheila Kanani
Text for Penguin Readers edition adapted by Anne Collins
Text copyright © Dr Shelia Kanani, 2019
Illustrated by Sarah Walsh
Illustrations copyright © Sarah Walsh, 2019
Illustrations page 4 (centre right, bottom left) and page 5 (centre right) by Amit Tayal

The moral right of the original author and the original illustrator has been asserted

Printed and bound in Great Britain by Clays Ltd, Elcograf S.p.A.

A CIP catalogue record for this book is available from the British Library

ISBN: 978-0-241-44738-3

All correspondence to
Penguin Books
Penguin Random House Children's
One Embassy Gardens, 8 Viaduct Gardens,
London SW11 7BW

Contents

People in the book

Michelle Obama

Melvinia

Michelle's mother, Marian, and father, Fraser

Michelle's brother, Craig

Michelle's husband, Barack

Michelle's daughters, Malia and Sasha

New words

basketball

date

graduate

mayor

piano

Note about the book

Michelle Obama has had an **extraordinary*** life – this means that her life has not been normal or "ordinary". She is strong, intelligent and she has done well at many things. She is a wife, a mother, and a **qualified lawyer**. From 2009–2017, she was First Lady of the United States, helping her famous husband, Barack Obama. But people don't only **admire** Michelle because she was the wife of a **president**. She has worked hard in **public services** and believes strongly that **education** is the most important thing in life. She thinks girls everywhere in the world must have an education, and very much admires the Pakistani schoolgirl, Malala Yousafzai. (*The Extraordinary Life of Malala Yousafzai* is also in Penguin Readers at level 2.) She has started many **campaigns**; she wants young people to be more **healthy** and to give them more **opportunities**. She wants to make the world a better place.

Before-reading questions

1 Look at the title and cover of this book. Describe the woman. Why is she famous? What do you know about her?
2 What information would you like to find out from the book?
3 How can the wife of a US president help her husband? Is her job hard or easy, do you think?
4 What do you know about the lives of other US presidents and their wives?

*Definitions of words in **bold** can be found in the glossary on pages 78–80.

CHAPTER ONE

The Robinson family

"I wake up in a house . . . Slaves built it. I watch my daughters — two beautiful, intelligent, black young women — go to school, waving goodbye to their father, the President of the United States, the son of a man from Kenya."
Michelle Obama

In 1850, a little girl called Melvinia was living in South Carolina, in the south east of the United States of America. Melvinia was six years old and she was a slave. Slaves did not have **free** lives. They worked for no money on plantations. These were enormous farms in the south of the USA.

Rich farmers owned the plantations and grew plants like sugar. They sold sugar to people in the north of the USA and other countries. But it was hard work to grow sugar, and the farmers needed a lot of people to work on their plantations.

Then some men started bringing slaves from Africa. They took men, women and children from their homes and put them on ships for America. When they got to America, the men sold them for a lot of money to the plantation farmers.

The slave ships were really terrible and the journey was long and hard. The men on the ships kept many slaves together and they could not move. The slaves were very frightened and they did not have enough to eat. Many slaves became ill and died. Sometimes the men hit them and threw them into the sea.

The first slaves came to Jamestown, Virginia, on a Dutch ship in 1619. In the next 200 years,

about 600,000 more slaves followed. Their life on the plantations was often very difficult. Some farmers were kind to their slaves, but many others did horrible things. They took children away from their parents, and sold them to other plantation farmers. For many farmers, their slaves were not like people, but like farm animals or things. The **laws** about slaves were very hard. Slaves could not leave their plantations.

A farmer called David Patterson owned Melvinia and twenty other slaves. Melvinia had to work very hard on Patterson's plantation. She did not go to school, and she could not read or write. After Patterson died in 1852, Melvinia went to work for his daughter, Christianne, and her husband.

They owned a plantation in Georgia, hundreds of miles away from Patterson's plantation in South Carolina. On Christianne's plantation, Melvinia was one of only three slaves. She was still only eight years old, but she had lots of things to do. She gave food to the cows, and **looked after** the sheep and plants. In 1859, when Melvinia was about fifteen, she had a baby. She called him Dolphus. Later, she had three more children on the plantation in Georgia.

In 1863, things began to change for African-American slaves in the United States. Abraham Lincoln, the president at that time, made a new law and after that, some slaves had free lives. Most of them had to **continue** working on the plantations, but now the farmers had to pay them. So Melvinia continued working on the farm in Georgia.

When she was in her thirties or forties, Melvinia went to find her old friends on the plantation in South Carolina. She came back to Kingston in Georgia with some of them and worked as a midwife, helping women to have babies.

Melvinia became a very important person in the **community** because of her job. She **shared** a home in Kingston with her adult children and also looked after her four grandchildren. Later, her son Dolphus married and started a family. Many years later, Dolphus's **great**-great-grandchildren went to live in Chicago.

The story of Melvinia's life was not very different from many other slave girls in America in the 1800s. But the life of her great-great-great-granddaughter has been **extraordinary**.

Michelle LaVaughn Robinson was born in the South Side of Chicago, Illinois, USA, on 17th January 1964. When Michelle was a child, she had a happy life. Her parents, Fraser and Marian, had ordinary jobs. Fraser worked for the city's **public services**, and Marian was a secretary for a clothes **firm**. Michelle's brother, Craig, was two years older than her. The family did not have much money, so their apartment had only one bedroom. Michelle and Craig shared the living room, but they made it into two rooms by putting a bed sheet in the centre.

The children were very lucky because their parents understood that **education** was very important. When she was a child, Marian wanted to be a children's doctor, but she never had the **opportunity** to go to college. She was from a large family and both her parents had to work hard. Her dad painted houses and her mum was a nurse. Marian wanted Craig and Michelle to have a good education, and taught them a lot at home. This gave Michelle and Craig a strong start in life, and both children could read when they were four.

They studied hard, but they always helped their mother with the housework too.

After the children were born, Marian stayed at home to look after them. Michelle's dad had multiple sclerosis, a terrible **illness**. People with this illness can have problems with their eyes, and moving their arms and legs. But Fraser's illness did not stop him from going to work every day. So the young Michelle learned that working hard is very important. Later, she said, "My father worked so hard to give us a home." She knew that the best way to help him was to study hard and make him **proud** of her.

The Robinsons had a lot of fun too. They sometimes enjoyed eating pizza on a Friday evening. On Saturdays, Michelle did jobs in the apartment like cleaning the bathroom, but on Sundays, the family went for long drives. In the evenings and at weekends, they played games, read books, and visited other people in the family. The Robinsons only **allowed** their children to watch one hour of TV every day. Michelle's favourite TV programme was *The Brady Bunch*. It was a funny programme about a large American family in the 1970s.

Michelle also remembers the long, fun days of summers, when the family went on holiday to White Cloud. This was a small town on the White River in Michigan.

Michelle's great-aunt Robbie lived downstairs from the Robinson family. Robbie was a strong, clever woman, and Michelle loved her very much. Perhaps she also learned some lessons for life from Robbie. Robbie was a student at Northwestern **University**. At night, the students had to sleep together in a dormitory, a large room with beds. But the university did not allow Robbie to sleep in the dormitory because she was black. Robbie was not happy about this, and she asked some **lawyers** to help her. In the end, the university had to pay her a lot of money.

Robbie also taught Michelle to play the piano and sing. Michelle loved playing the piano. She played it every day and every night. When she was a child, people often had to tell her to stop!

CHAPTER TWO
Top of the class

Michelle's first school was Bryn Mawr Elementary School in Chicago. In the USA, elementary school is children's first school. They usually begin when they are six years old, and they graduate when they are ten or eleven. After elementary school, children go to middle school and then to high school. High school usually begins at the age of fourteen, and students graduate when they are eighteen.

Michelle was a very clever girl. When she was eleven years old, she was already going to classes for very able students. After that, she became a student at the Whitney M. Young Magnet High School in Chicago. This was a wonderful opportunity for her.

A "magnet school" is a special school for top students. There are about 3,400 magnet schools in the USA today and 3.5 million magnet school students. The Whitney M. Young Magnet High School got its name from Whitney Moore Young

Jr., an important African-American **civil rights leader**. He worked very hard to make the lives of African Americans in the USA better.

The Whitney M. Young Magnet High School is open to all students in Chicago. It gives students from families without much money the opportunity for a good education. But it is not easy to study there. Students must have very good **grades**, and take a special exam before they can **join** the school.

Michelle's grades were excellent, and she did very well in the exam. The school was a long way from her home, and she had to travel more than two hours every day, but this did not matter to her. She was very happy at the school, and she worked hard. She joined a group of the top students at the school, studying on a special programme to get ready for college exams. She also did lots of things outside class, and looked after the money for an important student **organisation**. She was good at sports too, but (her brother Craig said) she did not like losing!

Michelle was very good at many things at school, but she was sometimes worried when things went wrong. For example, when she did not give the right answer to an exam question, she could not forget about it. Later, Michelle said: "I would love to go back in time and tell a younger Michelle, "These middle- and high-school years are just a very small part of your life, and all the small things and all those times when you were worried because you got one question wrong in that exam – none of that is important in the big picture of your life."

'For me, education was power.'

Michelle Obama

CHAPTER THREE

Higher education

While Michelle was at high school, she started thinking about going to a top university like Princeton University. Princeton is in the Ivy League – a group of the best universities in America. Princeton started in 1746 and is the fourth oldest university in the USA. At that time, it was called the College of New Jersey, but in 1896 its name changed to Princeton University.

Many important people have graduated from Princeton. Two of them became American presidents. James Madison, the fourth American president, graduated in 1771 and Woodrow Wilson, the 28th president, graduated in 1879. John F. Kennedy, the 35th American president, also went to Princeton, but after two months, he became ill and had to leave. Some famous actors and writers have also graduated from Princeton, and in 1973, Queen Noor of Jordan graduated from there.

The road to Princeton was not easy for Michelle. One of her teachers did not think she was clever enough to go there. But this did not stop Michelle. She worked even harder because she wanted to show everyone that her teacher was wrong. So she studied hard, joined more groups and tried to get better and better grades. In 1981, she got a place at Princeton, and graduated from Whitney Young with the title "Salutatorian" of her class. This was the name for the second-best graduate of a class.

Michelle was very excited to go to Princeton because she did not know anything about life at university. She only knew about living in a small apartment with her family. Neither of her parents went to university, so they could not tell her much about it.

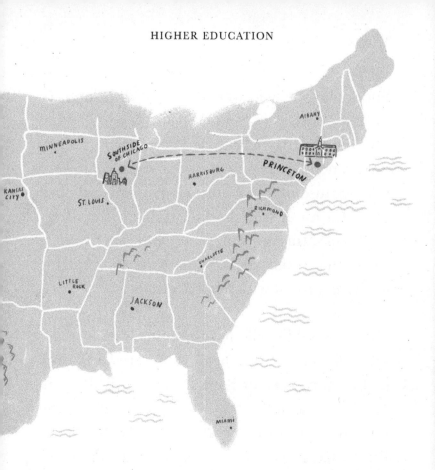

Princeton is nearly 800 miles east of Chicago. Michelle's brother, Craig, was already studying there. After Princeton, he became a basketball teacher at Oregon State University and Brown University, another university in the Ivy League. Later, he played basketball for the famous New York Knicks. When Michelle came to Princeton, people called her "Craig's little sis" (= younger sister).

Suddenly Michelle was a student at a large Ivy League university, and her life was changing. She mostly enjoyed life at Princeton University, but sometimes people showed **racism** towards her because of the colour of her skin. Michelle shared a room with a white student. But after a few weeks, this girl's mother wanted her to move to another room. She did not want her daughter to share a room with a black girl.

Sometimes Michelle felt the other students were very different from her. Many students drove to the university in their expensive BMW cars. Michelle's family did not have much money and she did not know any adults with a BMW. But because she was a student at Princeton, sometimes she felt that she was not part of her community at home either.

But usually, Michelle felt happy at Princeton. Most of the other students and teachers tried to understand her and they wanted her to do well. When Michelle was not happy about something, she always tried to change it.

Michelle questioned the way that the university taught French because there were not enough opportunities to practise speaking the language. She also joined a group of students called the Third World Center. These students were from **ethnic minorities**. As part of this group, Michelle ran the daycare centre. This centre helped to look after students' young children and also helped older children. Michelle and other students gave the children lessons after school and helped them with their schoolwork.

In her last year at Princeton, Michelle wrote a paper with the title "Princeton-Educated Blacks and the Black Community". She found four hundred ethnic minority graduates from Princeton and asked them lots of questions, but only ninety replied.

QUESTIONS FOR BLACK GRADUATES

- *How do you feel about being African-American?*

- *How did you feel before you started university?*

- *How did you feel after you graduated?*

- *Did you feel comfortable when you were a student?*

- *Do you think that the colour of your skin was important in your university life?*

Michelle studied hard at Princeton, and did very well there. She graduated in 1985 with a grade of *cum laude*, which means "top of the class".

After Princeton, Michelle went to law school at another top Ivy League university, Harvard University in Cambridge, Massachusetts. She graduated from Harvard University in 1988. While she was there, she started a **campaign** for the university to have more ethnic minority students and teachers. She also helped people without much money to find places to live.

When she graduated from Harvard, Michelle was a proud, well-educated young woman. She was very **confident** about herself and her abilities. She went back to her hometown of Chicago and got her first job with a law firm called Sidley Austin. She did not know it, but now her life was *really* going to change.

CHAPTER FOUR

Michelle meets Barack

Michelle was now twenty-five and already a **qualified** lawyer. She worked very hard in her job at Sidley Austin. When her mother asked her about boys, she said, "I'm not going to think about boys, only work!"

But one day in 1989, this all changed when a new young man joined Sidley Austin from law school. He was a twenty-seven-year-old student. He was still training to be a lawyer and he needed to learn about working in different law firms. His name was Barack Obama.

Sidley Austin asked Michelle to be Barack Obama's mentor. This meant that she had to work with him closely and take him everywhere. She had to teach him about the firm, and the jobs of its different lawyers. Michelle and Barack were two of only a few black people working for Sidley Austin at that time.

Michelle and Barack went to work and community meetings together, and they often had lunch with the firm's customers. Then Barack suddenly asked Michelle to go on a date with him, but she said no. She did not think it was right to go on a date because she was Barack's mentor and they were working together.

At first Michelle thought Barack had a big nose, but she slowly started to like him! She wanted to say yes to the date, but she also wanted to be sure that he was a good person. Craig always told her, "If you play basketball with someone, you can learn a lot about them." So she asked Barack to play basketball with Craig! After their game, Craig said a lot of good things about Barack, so Michelle agreed to go on a date with him.

On their first date, they saw a film called *Do the Right Thing*. The film was about racism in Brooklyn, New York. Then they went to get ice cream and they shared their first kiss outside a shopping centre.

Later, the owners of the shopping centre put a plate outside. It showed the place of Barack and Michelle's first kiss. On the plate are some words from Barack, saying, "On our first date, I bought her the finest ice cream from Baskin-Robbins. I kissed her, and it was like chocolate."

After two years, Barack finished his law exams and he became a qualified lawyer too. Michelle and Barack were very happy, and went out to dinner to have a good time. Then Michelle had a wonderful surprise. When they were finishing their meal, the waiter brought a ring for her from Barack! They got married in Chicago on 3rd October 1992, and danced to Stevie Wonder's "You and I" for their first dance.

In the next years, Michelle's life changed a lot. While she was working at Sidley Austin, she had big plans and ideas. She wanted to make the

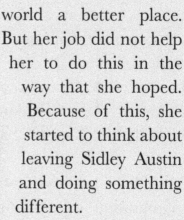

world a better place. But her job did not help her to do this in the way that she hoped. Because of this, she started to think about leaving Sidley Austin and doing something different.

In March 1991, her life changed again when her father's multiple sclerosis became worse and he died. Soon after this, a good friend of hers died from an illness too. Michelle felt very sad and she decided it was time to change her life and leave Sidley Austin.

Michelle decided that she wanted to work for the public services and help the community. For the next ten years, she did many different jobs and she was excellent at all of them. She worked for the mayor of Chicago and also worked for the student services at the University of Chicago. In this time, Barack and Michelle had two children. Their first daughter, Malia, was born in 1998, and Natasha (Sasha) was born in 2001.

Michelle's favourite job was working for an organisation called Public Allies. Two college graduates, Vanessa Kirsch and Katrina Browne, started Public Allies in 1992 in Washington, D.C. They wanted to show that young people can help to make a community better. The organisation trained young adults in different parts of the USA to become leaders in public services. These young

people were called "Allies" because they helped people in their communities. They worked for ten months in different places – for example, centres for people without homes, city offices and other workplaces. Some "Allies" were university and college students; others already had jobs.

In 1993, Michelle started Public Allies Chicago. She was their leader until 1996, and said, "I was never happier in my life than when I was working to build Public Allies."

Public Allies Chicago trained thirty to forty young people every year for jobs in **government** or public service organisations. Michelle had to work very hard, but she loved it. She had to do lots of different things. She had to get money for Public Allies, then find young people to join the

organisation and train them. Some "Allies" were university and college students from rich white families. But Michelle also found good young people from the poorest parts of Chicago. Some of these were black, some Asian and Hispanic. But they all wanted the same thing – to help the community.

Michelle met with important people in the city to ask them for money for Public Allies, but she was also happy to do boring jobs in the office. She was able to talk to everyone, from poor people to the mayor. She was always confident, and she was never afraid. One of the first young people in Public Allies Chicago, Jobi Petersen, said about her, "She had a way of making you feel that you could do anything."

Michelle learned many things from Public Allies about working in the community. She went on to help start another organisation in Chicago called the Community Service Center. This also gave students opportunities to work in public services in the city.

CHAPTER FIVE

The road to the White House

Barack Obama was now a qualified lawyer and he went on to teach law at the University of Chicago Law School from 1992 until 2004. But he was also very interested in getting a top job in **politics**. So he decided to start a campaign to get into the US Congress. Congress is part of the US government and it makes the laws for the country. It started in 1789, and has two "Houses" – the House of Representatives and the United States Senate. The people in the Senate are called senators.

There are 435 people in the House of Representatives and 100 people in the Senate. Each of the fifty states (= parts) in the USA sends people to the House of Representatives. The bigger states send more people than the smaller states. But every state sends two senators to the Senate. Congress meets in the Capitol building on Capitol Hill in Washington, D.C. – the most important city in the USA.

Michelle wanted to help Barack with his campaign to get into Congress. But she was also worried about her young daughters, Malia and Sasha. Michelle was an excellent mother, and she wanted to be with Malia and Sasha and look after them. But after Barack started his campaign, Michelle had to do many things away from her children to help her husband. She had to work hard to get money for the campaign. She also had to meet important people and give **interviews** to the **media**. She did not really enjoy doing these things, but she liked visiting people and seeing inside their houses!

Michelle was worried about her daughters.

In 1996, Barack became a senator in the Illinois Senate. But he still wanted to get into the US Congress. He started a campaign to get into the House of Representatives in 2000. He worked very hard at it, but he did not win. In 2002, he started another campaign. This time, things went better. In 2004, the people of Illinois chose Barack to go to the US Senate in Washington, D.C.

After this, the lives of the Obama family had to change. Barack had to be in Washington, D.C. most of the time. But it was a long way from Chicago, about 700 miles by road, and so Barack could not come home to his family every day after work. Michelle did not want the family to go to Washington. She felt it was important for Malia and Sasha to stay in Chicago. They were still very young and they did not know anybody in Washington. They might also not be happy at a new school with new people. So she decided it was best for Barack to go and live in Washington without his family. This meant that sometimes Michelle and the girls did not see Barack for weeks. But they talked on the phone a lot, and Barack visited them in Chicago as often as possible.

Michelle was a mother, but it was also important for her to keep working. When her younger daughter, Sasha, was only four months old, the University of Chicago Hospitals asked Michelle to go for a job interview. Michelle was very excited because this was a wonderful opportunity for her and she wanted the job very much. But she could not find anybody to look after Sasha while she was at the interview. So she took Sasha with her and Sasha slept in her car seat while the people interviewed Michelle. Michelle explained that her husband was away from home, and she could not leave her baby. The people liked Michelle because she was **honest** with them. Michelle thought, "Look, this is who I am. I've got a husband. He is away from home. I've got two little babies. They are the most important things in my life. If you want me to do the job, you have to pay me to do the job and you have to allow me to do it when I can."

Michelle did well in the interview and got the job. She worked for the University of Chicago Hospitals for seven years and became their **vice-president** in 2005.

Barack was also doing very well in his new life as a senator in Congress. He did many good things, and people liked him. In 2007, when Malia and Sasha were still under ten, he had a very important opportunity. He started a campaign for the top job in America – he wanted to be the president of the United States!

Barack had to work very hard on his campaign to be president and he needed Michelle to come to Washington, D.C. to help him. She agreed, but first Barack had to agree to do something for her. She said to him, "I will help you, but you have to stop smoking if you win!"

Barack agreed to stop smoking, so Michelle went to Washington, D.C. to be with him while her mother looked after Malia and Sasha in Chicago. Michelle helped Barack in many ways and she also became famous in America. People often saw her on the news or in interviews with the media. When people read about her or saw her on TV, they were often very surprised. She was strong and honest, and had many of her own ideas.

**Michelle worked hard to
help Obama with his campaign.**

At the start of Barack's campaign, Michelle talked a lot about family and education. These things were very important to her, and she believed in them very much. She didn't want people to think about her as just the wife of Barack Obama.

But by 2008, Michelle had no time for her own work. She once went to thirty-three places in eight days to help Barack with his campaign. She also worked with famous TV people like Oprah Winfrey. Like Michelle, Oprah is a strong, intelligent African-American woman with many of her own ideas. Oprah had a TV programme for twenty-five years, from 1986 to 2011, and some people have called her the "Queen of All Media". Millions of people in the USA enjoyed watching Oprah's programme every week.

But not everybody was happy with Michelle. Some people in the media started to say and write bad things about her. They called her an "angry black woman". These people said, "Michelle Obama is not interested in helping America. Other things are more important for her." Maybe these people were afraid of Michelle because she was very confident, honest and intelligent. Some people were also more interested in Michelle's hair and clothes than her ideas!

But Michelle was a strong woman, and she did not allow anyone to make her feel bad. She said, "When someone is not kind, you don't act in the same way . . . When they go low, we go high."

In the summer of 2008, the media started to say kinder things about Michelle. She did many interviews on TV programmes and on the evening news. More and more people listened to her ideas and began to understand her better.

CHAPTER SIX

The First Lady

Barack Obama won the race to be President of the United States in November 2008. In January 2009, the Obama family came to live in Washington, D.C. Their new home was the

White House. This is a very famous and important building because it is the president's office as well as his home. The address of the White House is 1600, Pennsylvania Avenue and its story is very interesting.

African slaves built many parts of the White House. They started work on the building in 1792, but it took eight years to finish it. There were problems with rainwater going into the stones of the building. The workmen were afraid that the stones were going to break, so they painted them with a special white paint. This stopped the rainwater. This white paint gives the building its famous name. The 26th American president, Theodore Roosevelt, first called it the White House in 1901.

The second US president, John Adams, started living in the White House with his family in 1800. But they were not happy because it was not a comfortable place to live. The rooms were very large and cold, and people had to walk for more than a mile to get water.

But when the Obama family moved into the White House, it was a warm and comfortable building. The White House has offices, rooms for the family and a library. But these rooms are not open to ordinary people. If you visit the White House, you can see the East Room, the Blue Room, the Green Room, the Red Room and the dining room.

In 1972, Pat Nixon, wife of the 37th US president, Richard Nixon, first opened the White House gardens to people. You can buy tickets twice a year, in spring and autumn, to walk around the gardens and **admire** their many beautiful plants.

When Barack Obama became president, Michelle became the First Lady of the United States (FLOTUS), the title of the wife of the president. The First Lady does not have one special job, but she has a lot of **power**. The public are usually very interested in the First Lady, and what she says and does – and her clothes! There have been some very famous First Ladies, like Jacqueline Kennedy, wife of the President John F. Kennedy.

While she was helping Barack in his campaign, Michelle learned many things about politics and government. But she wanted the American people to see her as a wife and mother too. People liked the Obamas because they did the same things as ordinary families. Michelle was the First Lady, but she also had two daughters. She enjoyed working in the garden and playing with her children and their two dogs, Sunny and Bo.

Michelle was rich and famous and many people admired her. But these were not the most important things in life for her. As First Lady, she helped her husband with his ideas and campaigns. She was happy to do this, but she also wanted to use her power to fight for other things. The public services were still very important for her, and she wanted to continue working for them. Some poor people did not have anywhere to live, and she helped to find homes for them.

There were soup kitchens near the White House. These kitchens gave free soup to hungry people with no money to buy food. Michelle visited the kitchens and helped to give people lunch. She asked the ordinary American people to give food too, or just come and help. At the same time, she tried to learn more about the US government, and houses and education in America.

Michelle was also worried because many American children were becoming **obese**. They ate the wrong foods, and they did not do enough sports like running, swimming or riding a bicycle. Michelle wanted to help children look after their bodies better. So in 2010, she started the "Let's Move!" campaign. This campaign helped children to eat **healthy** foods and do more sports.

Michelle had an excellent idea for the campaign. She asked Beyoncé, the famous African-American singer and songwriter, to be part of "Let's Move!" too. Many children liked Beyoncé and wanted to be like her, so they became very interested in the campaign. Beyoncé sang a song called "Move Your Body" and she made a video to go with it.

In the video, Beyoncé wears bright clothes and dances with children in a normal school dining room at lunchtime. The children have lots of fun dancing with Beyoncé, and running and jumping in the dining room. Michelle was very happy with the video. Many children across the USA watched it, and wanted to dance like Beyoncé too.

Michelle hopes that in 2030, there will be fewer obese children in the USA. While she was First Lady, she also started a White House Kitchen Garden, and grew fresh fruit and vegetables for her family and people visiting the White House.

In 2011, Michelle started another campaign called "Joining **Forces**". She did this together with Jill Biden, the wife of Joe Biden – Barack Obama's vice-president. Jill was the Second Lady of the United States. Like Michelle, Jill was very interested in helping people through education. She taught English and reading in high schools for thirteen years. After that she taught in different colleges.

Michelle and Jill started the "Joining Forces" campaign to help veterans – people who worked in the **military** when they were younger. Many veterans had problems when they left the military because they could not find ordinary jobs easily. Things were difficult for them in other ways too because many of them saw terrible things when they were in the military. Life for these men and women was very different from the lives of other people.

When Michelle heard about these people's problems, she often cried because some of their stories were very sad. So Michelle and Jill wanted to help veterans find good jobs, and give them the opportunity for a better life. Michelle also wanted the American people to learn more about life in the military so they could understand and help the veterans more.

Some people in the United States were still against Michelle, because they were not happy with her work. They thought she was wrong to start campaigns to help obese children and veterans. They wanted her to do more things to

Michelle helped many veterans.

help women. Michelle wanted to help women, and as many different groups of people as she could. She could never make everybody happy; she just wanted to do her best.

Michelle enjoys speaking to lots of different people. She has travelled all over the world and met many world leaders, for example, Queen Elizabeth II in London, the Pope, the King of Saudi Arabia and Nelson Mandela. When she visits a new place, she often speaks to the people there. She has spoken at universities and **political** and sports meetings. She is never afraid to speak.

When Barack Obama was president, he spoke to the American people every week on the radio. Most presidents before him did the same thing. But one day in 2014, just before Mother's Day, Americans had a big surprise. It was not Barack speaking to them, it was Michelle!

**Michelle met
Queen Elizabeth of England.**

CHAPTER SEVEN

A voice for young girls

On the night of 14th April 2014, a terrible thing happened to hundreds of schoolgirls in Nigeria. Men from a group called Boko Haram came and took them because they wanted to stop the girls getting an education. The men kept the girls in secret places. This was really terrible for their parents and families. Where were their daughters? What was going to happen to them? Were they dead?

Michelle and Barack felt very sad and angry about the girls and their families because they too had young daughters. They were worried because they knew that the same thing could happen in other countries.

When she spoke on the radio to the American people, Michelle said, "What happened in Nigeria . . . is a story we see every day as girls around the world have terrible problems to get an education." Then she continued, "I want you to know that Barack has told our government to do everything possible to help the Nigerian government to find these girls and bring them home. In these girls, Barack and I see our own daughters."

Michelle started a campaign called "Bring Back Our Girls" to help the Nigerian schoolgirls. Earlier in the week, she went on Twitter and showed a picture of herself holding a piece of paper with the words #Bring Back Our Girls. Later she made a video about them for YouTube – but many of the girls did not come back.

Many people admire Michelle because she is a strong, confident and intelligent woman. But it is sadly true that sometimes the media have been more interested in her clothes than in her work! Yes, she is famous because she is the wife of the president, but she has always tried to use this in a good way to help people. If you are famous, people are interested in you and some of them want to be like you. People listen to you and follow you, so you can **reach** and change many lives.

Michelle wants all young people to understand about education. It has always been very important to her, because it gives all young people the opportunity for a better life. She started another campaign called "Reach Higher!" in 2014. This campaign had a very strong and important message for young people – that they must continue their education after high school. Michelle said, "You have to stay in school. You have to. You have to go to college . . . because people can never take your education away from you."

In 2015, Michelle and Barack Obama started the "Let Girls Learn" campaign. Michelle understood that women in America and Europe were lucky, but girls in many other countries had a lot of problems getting an education. She wanted to help these girls as much as possible. Michelle had an excellent education because she was clever and worked hard at school. So she wanted all girls to have the same opportunity for a good education.

On 11th October 2013 Michelle, Barack and their daughter Malia met Malala Yousafzai. Malala was sixteen years old and was born in Pakistan in 1997. She had two younger brothers and her father was a teacher. Many Pakistani girls do not go to school, but Malala loved learning and her father was very happy for her to get an education. Malala learned three languages and she was hoping to become a teacher or a doctor.

But when Malala was about ten years old, a group of men called the Taliban came to her village. They did not allow women to work and they wanted to stop girls from getting an education. So they closed all the girls' schools.

Malala and her father were very sad and angry about the Taliban. Malala wanted to tell the world her story, and she talked to some people from the news. "The Taliban are very dangerous," she said. Then a British news organisation asked Malala to write about the Taliban. Malala used a different name and sent her work to the organisation in secret. Soon, people all over the world were reading Malala's story about the Taliban.

When the Taliban heard about this, they were very angry with Malala. Later, the government changed and the schools opened again. But the

Taliban did not forget about Malala. On 9th October 2012, after school, she was going home on a bus. Suddenly two men from the Taliban got onto the bus. One was carrying a gun and asked "Who is Malala?" When he found her, he pointed the gun at her and **shot** her in the head.

Malala did not die, but she was very ill. A doctor from a hospital in Birmingham, a city in England, was there in Pakistan. He heard about Malala and took her to England. She woke up a week later in a hospital in Birmingham. At first, she was surprised and frightened. She understood that she was not in Pakistan, because everybody was speaking English! But where was this strange place and how did she get there?

Then the nurses explained everything to her. She understood that she was in England, thousands of miles away from her home in Pakistan. The doctors and nurses looked after her well, and after three months, Malala left the hospital in Birmingham. She could not see, hear or walk very well, but six months later, she was back at school in Pakistan.

'ONE CHILD,
one teacher,
ONE BOOK
and one pen
CAN CHANGE
the world.

Malala Yousafzai

On her sixteenth birthday, Malala spoke to the United Nations, the famous world organisation in New York. "I want all girls to have the opportunity for education," she said. In 2013, she wrote a book called *I Am Malala*. Today, people all over the world know her story. After Michelle met Malala, she said, "A man shot Malala in the head just for trying to go to school. There are tens of millions of girls like Malala in every corner of the world and they are not in school – girls who are so intelligent, hard-working and hungry to learn."

In 2016, Michelle and Oprah Winfrey talked on Oprah's TV programme for an hour about women's problems in America. Michelle wanted to give women the message, "The most important person in your life is you."

Michelle was very proud of her two daughters, Malia and Sasha. While the family were living in the White House, she said, "I wake up in a house . . . Slaves built it. I watch my daughters – two beautiful, intelligent, black young women – go to school, waving goodbye to their father, the President of the United States, the son of a man from Kenya. His father came here to America to get an education and get better opportunities in life."

**Michelle was very proud of
her two daughters.**

Life after the White House

Barack Obama became President of the United States in January 2009. In America, a person cannot be president for longer than eight years. If the people are not happy with the president, after four years they have the opportunity to choose another one. But Barack and Michelle were working hard and doing well, and the American people liked them. So in 2012 they chose Barack to be president for the next four years too.

But when Barack's second four years finished in 2016, the race began for a new president. The American people had to choose between Donald Trump and Hillary Clinton.

Hillary Clinton was First Lady in 1993 when her husband, Bill Clinton, was the 42nd president. In 2016, Hillary started a campaign to be the first woman president. Michelle wanted Hillary to win very much. She spoke about her a lot and helped her as much as she could. But in November 2016, the people of the USA chose Donald Trump to be the new president.

It was the end of life in the White House for the Obamas. But Michelle was not sad to leave their famous home. This was not the end of her hopes and plans to make the world a better place. Michelle never wants to be a president of the United States. She wants to do things her own way.

When the Obamas left the White House, Michelle wanted to continue working for public services in the community, and also do more things with her daughters. Sasha was just a little girl of seven when Barack became president and the family moved to the White House. Michelle was happy because now the girls could have a more "ordinary" life, away from the media. She was happy about her own life too. She felt more free because the media were not so interested in her any more. When she was still First Lady, she said, "It's possible that many more people will be able to hear my voice after I leave the White House. They can't hear me now because I'm still Michelle Obama, the First Lady."

Michelle has continued her campaigns for **health** and education. For her, not having an education is "the most important civil rights problem that we have today."

The Obamas are still working hard, but they also enjoy travelling, visiting friends and family and living their lives away from the media. Their daughter Malia has gone to Harvard University, just like her mother.

Michelle has written a book about her life called *Becoming*. It is in three parts – "Becoming Me", "Becoming Us" and "Becoming More". The first part is about her early life and education, and ends with her first job at Sidley Austin when she met Barack Obama. The second part is about Barack's campaigns in politics, and ends when the American people chose him to be president. The third part is about the Obamas' family life in the White House. *Becoming* sold about 725,000 books in the USA and Canada on its first day and 1.4 million in its first week. After fifteen days, it became the best-selling book in the USA in 2018.

Michelle Obama is an extraordinary woman. She came from living in a small apartment with just two rooms, and has become many different things – a wife, a mother, a lawyer and First Lady of the United States. Today Michelle is still working very hard to make life better for young people all across the world.

TIMELINE

17th January 1964
Michelle is born.

1970
Michelle becomes a student first at Bryn Mawr Elementary School (1970–1977) then Whitney M. Young Magnet High School (1977–1981).

1985
Michelle graduates from Princeton University.

1988
Michelle graduates from Harvard Law School and joins the Sidley Austin law firm.

1989
She meets Barack Obama. They go on their first date.

1992
Michelle marries Barack Obama.

1993
Michelle started Public Allies Chicago.

1998 and 2001
Michelle and Barack's daughters, Malia and Sasha, are born.

2009
Barack becomes President of the United States and Michelle becomes First Lady (FLOTUS).

2010 - 2015
Michelle starts a number of campaigns: "Let's Move!", "Joining Forces", "Reach Higher!" and "Let Girls Learn".

2017
The Obama family leave the White House.

During-reading questions

Write the answers to these questions in your notebook.

CHAPTER ONE

1 How did slaves first come to America?
2 Who was Melvinia? Why is she important to Michelle?
3 How did Craig and Michelle's parents give their children a
   strong start in life?

CHAPTER TWO

1 Who was Whitney Moore Young Jr.?
2 How can children join the Whitney M. Young Magnet School?
3 Do you think Michelle enjoyed her years at high school?

CHAPTER THREE

1 Why did Michelle sometimes feel different from other
   students at Princeton University?
2 Who did she help when she was a student at Princeton?
3 Where did she go after she left Princeton?

CHAPTER FOUR

1 Why did Craig play basketball with Barack Obama?
2 Why did Michelle leave Sidley Austin?
3 What was Public Allies? Why do you think it was important
   to Michelle?

CHAPTER FIVE

1 How did Michelle help Barack with his campaign to get
   into the US Congress?
2 Why did Barack's family not go to Washington, D.C. too?
3 Who called Michelle "an angry black woman"? How do you
   think she felt about this?

CHAPTER SIX

1 How did the White House get its name?
2 Why did Michelle start the "Let's Move!" campaign?
3 What did she do to help US veterans?

CHAPTER SEVEN

1 Why did Michelle speak on the radio in April 2014?
2 Who is Malala Yousafzai? What happened to her?
3 Why is this chapter called "A voice for young girls"?

CHAPTER EIGHT

1 Who did Michelle want to be president after Barack?
2 How did she feel about leaving the White House?
3 What does Michelle think is the most important civil rights problem today?

After-reading questions

1 What did you learn about
   a the White House
   b Barack Obama
   c Michelle's life as First Lady?
2 What things do you want to say to a "younger you"?
3 "It's possible that many more people will be able to hear my voice after I leave the White House." Why does Michelle say this?
4 Would you like to read Michelle's book, *Becoming*? Why/Why not?
5 Do you agree that Michelle's life has been extraordinary? Why/Why not?

Exercises

CHAPTER ONE

1 **Match the two parts of the sentences in your notebook.**
Example: 1 – d

1 Melvinia had to look after
2 In 1863, Abraham Lincoln made
3 Michelle's dad worked
4 Michelle learned it was important
5 The Robinson family had
6 The university paid a lot of money

a for the public services.
b to work hard.
c a happy life together.
d plants and animals on the farm.
e to Michelle's great-aunt Robbie.
f a new law about slaves.

CHAPTER TWO

2 **Write the correct word in your notebook.**
1 Children in the USA go first to *elementary* / **high** school.
2 They usually **begin** / **graduate** from high school at the age of eighteen.
3 Michelle worked hard and got excellent **grades** / **sports.**
4 Magnet schools give poorer children the **opportunity** / **organisation** for a better education.
5 If children want to **add** / **join** a magnet school, they must take a special exam.
6 Michelle was **never** / **sometimes** worried when she gave the wrong answer in an exam.

3 Are these sentences *true* or *false*? Write the correct answers in your notebook.

1 Most American presidents went to Princeton.

False. Only two American presidents went to Princeton.

2 When Princeton University began, it had a different name.

3 The title "Salutatorian" means "top of the class".

4 Michelle did not want to go to Princeton.

5 Michelle had her own room when she started at Princeton.

6 The Third World Center helped children after school.

7 When Michelle left Princeton, she got her first job.

8 Sidley Austin was a law firm in Chicago.

CHAPTER FOUR

4 Complete these sentences in your notebook, using the words from the box.

mentor	community	date	confident
illness	qualified	organisation	basketball

1 At the age of twenty-five, Michelle was a *qualified* lawyer.

2 Michelle was Barack's ...., so she had to work closely with him.

3 Craig played a game of .... with Barack.

4 On their first ...., Michelle and Barack ate Baskin-Robbins ice cream.

5 In March 1991, Michelle's dad died from an ....

6 Public Allies was the name of an ....

7 Young people joined Public Allies because they wanted to help the ....

8 Michelle was a strong and .... young woman.

5 **Complete these sentences with the correct form of the verb.**

1 Queen Noor of Jordan *graduated* / **was graduating** from Princeton in 1973.

2 When Michelle first went to Princeton, her brother **was studying / studied** there.

3 In her last year at Princeton, Michelle **wrote / has written** a paper about black graduates.

4 When she was working at Sidley Austin, she **was meeting / met** a new young man.

5 When Barack Obama joined Sidley Austin, he **was training / trained** to be a lawyer.

6 Michelle **was starting / started** Public Allies Chicago.

6 **Put the sentences in the correct order in your notebook.**

a .... Barack decides to run for president.

b .... Barack gets into the US Congress as a senator.

c .... The Obama family start living in the White House.

d .... The American people choose Barack to be president.

e .... Michelle goes to Washington, D.C. to be with Barack and help with his campaigns.

f .... Barack lives in Washington, D.C. without his family.

g .... Michelle started the "Let's Move!" campaign.

h .....*1*..... Barack became a senator in the Illinois Senate.

CHAPTER SIX

7 Complete the information for the campaigns, using the words from the box.

> healthy foods   veterans   obese children
> job opportunities   do more sports   leaving the military
> Jill Biden   Beyoncé

"Let's Move!" campaign	"Joining Forces" campaign
1 _healthy foods_	5 ....
2	6 ....
3	7 ....
4	8 ....

CHAPTER SEVEN

8 Write the correct answers in your notebook.

1 Michelle spoke on the radio about _the Nigerian schoolgirls_ .
  a Malala Yousafzai.
  b the Nigerian schoolgirls.
  c education for young people.

2 The message of the "Reach Higher!" campaign was for
  a young girls only.
  b young people at school.
  c university teachers.

3 Malala Yousafzai's father wanted her to
  a stay at home.
  b fight the Taliban.
  c go to school.

4 On her sixteenth birthday, Malala
  a began writing a book.
  b started studying to be a doctor.
  c spoke to the United Nations.

CHAPTER EIGHT

9 Put the words in the correct order to make sentences in your notebook.

1 years. / Obama / for / president / eight / was / Barack
Barack Obama was president for eight years.

2 way. / Michelle / to / things / her / wants / own / do

3 continued / work / to / She / hard / the / for / has / community.

4 and / Obamas / visiting / The / and / enjoy / family. / travelling / friends

5 want / people / her / Michelle's / about / to / Many / read / life. / book

6 book, / part / the / Barack / president. / In / becomes / the / second / of

CHAPTERS ONE TO EIGHT

10 Complete these sentences in your notebook, using the names from the box.

Jill Biden	Oprah Winfrey	Marian Robinson
Beyoncé	Hillary Clinton	Michelle Obama

1 *Hillary Clinton* wanted to be the first woman US president.

2 .... wrote a book called *Becoming*.

3 .... wanted to be a children's doctor but was not able to go to college.

4 .... became the Second Lady of the US in 2009.

5 .... had a famous TV programme for twenty-five years.

6 .... made a video to help one of Michelle's campaigns.

Project work

1 Look online and find out about a famous political building in your country or another country. Write a newspaper report about it. Think about:
   a where it is
   b who built it, when and why
   c what it looks like
   d what happens there

2 Choose a person from one of these groups:
   a US presidents
   b First Ladies
   c famous black Americans
   Look online and find out more about them. Write a paragraph about their lives.

3 You are Oprah Winfrey and you are going to interview Michelle Obama about her life. Write five questions that you would like to ask her.

Glossary

admire (v.)
to like someone because you think they are a special person or because they are good at something

allow (v.)
to say that someone can do something

campaign (n.)
You start a *campaign* with other people because you want something to happen or because you want to make people's lives better.

civil rights (n.)
the things that everyone must be *allowed* to have, or be able to do, in their lives

community (n.)
a group of people. These people all live in the same place.

confident (adj.)
You are *confident* when you know that you can do things very well.

continue (v.)
to not stop doing something, or to start doing something again after stopping it

education (n.); **educated** (adj.)
when you learn about things. An *educated* or *well-educated* person has had a good education and learned a lot.

ethnic minority (n.)
a group of people in a country. They are different from most people in a country, for example, because they might be a different colour, speak a different language, etc.

extraordinary (adj.)
very different and much better than *ordinary* (= normal, and not special or different)

firm (n.)
A *firm* usually makes or sells things.

force (n.)
a large group of soldiers. A *force* fights on the ground, in the air or on water.

free (adj.)
A *free* person can go where they want and do what they want. Something is also *free* when you do not have to pay money for it.

government (n.)
a group of important people. They say what must happen in a country.

grade (n.)
A *grade* is a number or letter for your work at school. It shows if your work is good or not.

great- (adj.)
great- is a word for people in your family. For example, your *great-*aunt is the aunt of your mother or father. Your *great-great-*grandchildren are the children of your son or daughter's grandchildren.

health (n.); **healthy** (adj.)
Your *health* is how your body feels. *Healthy* food is good for you.

honest (adj.)
An *honest* person says true things. They are usually a good person.

illness (n.)
when you have something wrong with your body and you are not very well

interview (n.)
In an interview, someone asks you questions to decide if you will get a job. An *interview* is also when someone from a television programme or §newspaper asks you questions.

join (v.)
to do something with other people. It is also when you start going to a school, college, etc.

law (n.); **lawyer** (n.)
The *law* is the right and wrong things to do in a country. A *lawyer* helps people with the *law*.

leader (n.)
People listen to a *leader*, and they do the things their *leader* tells them to do.

look after (v.)
to help a person, an animal or a plant

mayor (n.)
the most important person in a town or city

media (n.)
the people working for a television programme, newspaper, etc.

military (n.)
the *military* is a country's soldiers

obese (adj.)
very fat

opportunity (n.)
when you can do a new and exciting thing

organisation (n.)
a group of people. They work together to do something.

politics (n.); **political** (adj.)
politics is the work of a government. *Political* is about the work of a *government*.

power (n.)
You have *power* when you can tell people to do something and they will do it.

president (n.)
the most important person in the *government* of countries without a king or queen

proud (adj.)
You are *proud* when you think that you or your family or friends have done well.

public services (n.)
work that helps people

qualified (adj.)
You are *qualified* when you pass an exam to do a job.

racism (n.)
when you think someone is not as good as you because they are a different colour

reach (v.)
You *reach* people when they listen to the things you say.

share (v.)
to use or do something with another person

shoot (past tense *shot*) (v.)
to use a gun because you want to hurt or kill someone

university (n.)
People can study at a *university* when they have left school.

vice-president (n.)
an important person. They help the *president* and do the president's job when he or she cannot do it. A vice-president is also an important person in a business.